United States Government Accountability Office

Report to the Honorable Jon Tester, U.S. Senate

April 2013

BORDER SECURITY

Partnership Agreements and Enhanced Oversight Could Strengthen Coordination of Efforts on Indian Reservations

G A O
Accountability ★ Integrity ★ Reliability

GAO-13-352

April 2013

BORDER SECURITY

Partnership Agreements and Enhanced Oversight Could Strengthen Coordination of Efforts on Indian Reservations

Why GAO Did This Study

Individuals seeking to enter the United States illegally may attempt to avoid screening procedures at ports of entry by crossing the border in areas between these ports, including Indian reservations, many of which have been vulnerable to illicit cross-border threat activity, such as drug smuggling, according to DHS. GAO was asked to review DHS's efforts to coordinate border security activities on Indian reservations. This report examines DHS's efforts to coordinate with tribal governments to address border security threats and vulnerabilities on Indian reservations. GAO interviewed DHS officials at headquarters and conducted interviews with eight tribes, selected based on factors such as proximity to the border, and the corresponding DHS field offices that have a role in border security for these Indian reservations. While GAO cannot generalize its results from these interviews to all Indian reservations and field offices along the border, they provide examples of border security coordination issues. This is a public version of a sensitive report that GAO issued in December 2012. Information that DHS, the Department of Justice (DOJ) and the Department of the Interior (DOI) deemed sensitive has been redacted.

What GAO Recommends

GAO recommends that DHS examine the benefits of government-to-government agreements with tribes and develop and implement a mechanism to monitor border security coordination efforts with tribes. DHS concurred with our recommendations.

View GAO-13-352. For more information, contact Rebecca Gambler at (202) 512-8777 or gamblerr@gao.gov

What GAO Found

The Department of Homeland Security (DHS) is coordinating in a variety of ways with tribes, such as through joint operations and shared facilities and Operation Stonegarden—a DHS grant program intended to enhance coordination among local, tribal, territorial, state, and federal law enforcement agencies in securing United States borders. However, the Border Patrol and tribes face coordination challenges. Officials from five tribes reported information-sharing challenges with the Border Patrol, such as not receiving notification of federal activity on their lands. Border Patrol officials reported challenges navigating tribal rules and decisions. Border Patrol and DHS have existing agreements with some, but not all, tribes to address specific border security issues, such as for the establishment of a law enforcement center on tribal lands. These agreements could serve as models for developing additional agreements between the Border Patrol and other tribes on their specific border security coordination challenges. Written government-to-government agreements could assist Border Patrol and tribal officials with enhancing their coordination, consistent with practices for sustaining effective coordination. DHS established an office to coordinate the components' tribal outreach efforts, which has taken actions such as monthly teleconferences with DHS tribal liaisons to discuss tribal issues and programs, but does not have a mechanism for monitoring and overseeing outreach efforts, consistent with internal control standards. Such monitoring should be performed continually; ingrained in the agency's operations; and clearly documented in directives, policies, or manuals to help ensure operations are carried out as intended. Implementing an oversight mechanism could help enhance DHS's department-wide awareness of and accountability for border security coordination efforts with the tribes while identifying those areas that work well and any needing improvement.

Contents

Abbreviations

BEST	Border Enforcement Security Task Force
BIA	Bureau of Indian Affairs
CBP	U.S. Customs and Border Protection
CBP-OFO	CBP Office of Field Operations
DHS	Department of Homeland Security
DOI	Department of the Interior
DOJ	Department of Justice
FEMA	Federal Emergency Management Agency
FMFIA	Federal Managers' Financial Integrity Act of 1982
HSI	Homeland Security Investigations
I&A	Intelligence and Analysis
IBET	Integrated Border Enforcement Team
ICE	U.S. Immigration and Customs Enforcement
IGA	Office of Intergovernmental Affairs
LEC	Law Enforcement Center
MOA	memorandum of agreement
OMB	Office of Management and Budget
ONDCP	Office of National Drug Control Policy
OSLTC	Office of State, Local and Tribal Coordination
POE	port of entry
THSGP	Tribal Homeland Security Grant Program
USCG	United States Coast Guard

United States Government Accountability Office
Washington, DC 20548

April 5, 2013

The Honorable Jon Tester
United States Senate

Dear Senator Tester:

The United States shares over 5,000 miles of border with Canada, and over 1,900 miles of border with Mexico. Individuals seeking to enter the United States illegally or to smuggle contraband may attempt to avoid the Department of Homeland Security's (DHS) U.S. Customs and Border Protection (CBP) screening procedures at ports of entry (POE) by crossing the borders in areas between POEs, including Indian reservations on the borders.[1] Eighty-six miles of the northern border and 68 miles of the southwest border are on 13 Indian reservations, many of which are vulnerable to illicit cross-border threat activity, such as drugs, weapons, and human smuggling, according to DHS officials.[2] As a result, the security of Indian reservations is a key part of the overall integrity of U.S. borders.

The United States has a unique legal and political relationship with Indian tribal governments, established through and confirmed by the Constitution of the United States, treaties, statutes, executive orders, and judicial decisions. In recognition of that special relationship, executive agencies have been charged with engaging in regular and meaningful consultation and collaboration with tribal officials in the development of federal policies that have tribal implications, and are responsible for strengthening the government-to-government relationships between the United States and

---

[1]Ports of entry are government-designated locations where CBP inspects persons and goods to determine whether they may be lawfully admitted or entered into the country. An Indian reservation is an area established by or pursuant to a treaty, statute, regulation, executive order, or other formal government recognition.

[2]A vulnerability is a physical feature or operational attribute that renders an entity open to exploitation or susceptible to a given hazard. A threat is a natural or man-made occurrence, individual, entity, or action that has or indicates the potential to harm life, information, operations, the environment, or property.

Indian tribes.[3] Securing U.S. borders is the primary responsibility of various components within DHS, in collaboration with other federal, state, local, and tribal entities. CBP, a component within DHS, is the frontline agency responsible for preventing terrorists and their weapons of terrorism from entering the United States and interdicting persons and contraband crossing the border illegally. The Border Patrol is the CBP component charged with carrying out this mission along border areas between the POEs.

As part of this mission, Border Patrol agents operate on Indian reservations on or near the border. U.S. Immigration and Customs Enforcement (ICE), also within DHS, is responsible for investigating the sources of cross-border crimes and dismantling illegal operations, including on Indian reservations. According to the 2012 through 2016 Border Patrol Strategic Plan, homeland security missions—such as border security missions—are conducted through collaboration with an array of homeland security partners, including state, local, tribal, and territorial governments. In May 2011, DHS issued a Tribal Consultation Policy to, among other things, promote border security coordination on Indian reservations.

You asked us to review federal collaboration with tribal governments on border security issues. In response, this report addresses the following question: To what extent is DHS coordinating with tribal governments to address border security threats and vulnerabilities on Indian reservations?

This report is a public version of the prior sensitive report that we provided to you. DHS, the Department of Justice (DOJ), and the Department of the Interior (DOI) deemed some of the information in the prior report as law enforcement sensitive, which must be protected from public disclosure. Therefore, this report omits sensitive information regarding a question about border security threats and vulnerabilities, as

---

[3]"Policies that have tribal implications" refers to regulations, legislative comments or proposed legislation, and other policy statements or actions that have substantial direct effects on one or more Indian tribes, on the relationship between the federal government and Indian tribes, or on the distribution of power and responsibilities between the federal government and Indian tribes. "Indian tribe" means an Indian or Alaska Native tribe, band, nation, pueblo, village, or community that the Secretary of the Interior acknowledges to exist as an Indian tribe pursuant to the Federally Recognized Indian Tribe List Act of 1994, 25 U.S.C. § 479a.

well as the names and locations of the Indian tribes and reservations within the review, and techniques used to carry out border security missions. Although the information provided in this report is more limited in scope, the overall methodology used for both reports is the same.

To determine the extent to which DHS is coordinating with tribes to address border security threats and vulnerabilities, we reviewed federal strategies, such as DHS's Northern Border Strategy, and policies and plans, such as DHS's Plan of Action to Develop a Tribal Consultation and Coordination Policy, which address coordination with tribal governments. In reviewing coordination between the federal government and tribal governments, we focused primarily on DHS's Office of Intergovernmental Affairs Tribal Desk (Tribal Desk)—DHS's designated lead for tribal relations and consultation—and the Border Patrol—the lead federal agency charged with securing the border in areas between the ports of entry—where the Indian reservations in our review are located. We reviewed DHS's Tribal Consultation and Coordination Plan, our prior work on effective interagency collaboration, and our *Standards for Internal Control in the Federal Government* to assess DHS's efforts to oversee and monitor coordination with tribes on border security.[4] Additionally, to determine the benefits and challenges regarding coordination between the governments, we conducted interviews with tribal officials such as chairmen and police chiefs, from eight different Indian reservations along the northern and southwest borders, selected based on their proximity to the borders according to U.S. Census data.[5] We also interviewed headquarters officials at DHS, DOJ, and DOI, to obtain information on their efforts related to border security on Indian reservations. We conducted interviews with officials from 10 Border Patrol stations, 7 Border Patrol sectors responsible for patrolling the Indian reservations in

---

[4]GAO, *Results-Oriented Government: Practices That Can Help Enhance and Sustain Collaboration among Federal Agencies*, GAO-06-15 (Washington D.C.: Oct. 21, 2005), and *Standards for Internal Control in the Federal Government*, GAO/AIMD-00-21.3.1 (Washington, D.C.: November 1999). These standards, issued pursuant to the requirements of the Federal Managers' Financial Integrity Act of 1982 (FMFIA), provide the overall framework for establishing and maintaining internal control in the federal government. Also pursuant to FMFIA, the Office of Management and Budget (OMB) issued Circular A-123, revised December 21, 2004, to provide the specific requirements for assessing the reporting on internal controls. Internal control standards and the definition of internal control in OMB Circular A-123 are based on GAO's *Standards for Internal Control in the Federal Government*.

[5]We did not review reservations on the U.S. border between Canada and Alaska.

our review,[6] and various other entities involved in border security on Indian reservations, including seven state and major urban area fusion centers,[7] two Border Enforcement Security Task Forces (BEST),[8] and three Integrated Border Enforcement Teams (IBETs).[9] While we cannot generalize information obtained from these interviews to all Indian reservations and federal agencies' field units along the northern and southwest borders, we selected these tribes and locations to provide examples of the way federal agencies coordinate with tribal governments on border security issues.

We conducted this performance audit from January 2012 to April 2013 in accordance with generally accepted government auditing standards. Those standards require that we plan and perform the audit to obtain sufficient, appropriate evidence to provide a reasonable basis for our findings and conclusions based on our audit objectives. We believe that the evidence obtained provides a reasonable basis for our findings and conclusions based on our audit objectives.

---

[6]The Border Patrol is organized into 20 sectors—with 8 sectors on the northern border, 9 sectors on the southwest border, and 3 sectors on coastal areas along the Gulf of Mexico and in Puerto Rico. Each sector has a headquarters with management personnel and various numbers of stations with agents responsible for patrolling within defined geographical areas. For example, the Tucson sector includes the Ajo, Casa Grande, Douglas, Naco, Nogales, Sonoita, Tucson, and Willcox stations.

[7]A fusion center is a collaborative effort of two or more agencies that provide resources, expertise, and information to the center with the goal of maximizing the ability to detect, prevent, investigate, and respond to criminal and terrorism activity.

[8]BESTs are task forces developed and facilitated by ICE to enhance border security, investigate transnational smuggling organizations, and combat violence related to smuggling occurring at the nation's borders, through coordinated colocated efforts. Partners involved include DHS Information and Analysis, CBP, the U.S. Coast Guard, the Drug Enforcement Administration, the Canadian Border Services Agency, and the Royal Canadian Mounted Police along with other key federal, state, tribal, and local law enforcement agencies.

[9]IBETs are permanent binational forums established through a charter that outlines partners' responsibilities for sharing border security information and coordinating cross-border law enforcement and antiterrorism efforts between the ports of entry. Core IBET agencies include Canada's Royal Canadian Mounted Police, the Canada Border Services Agency, CBP, ICE, and the Coast Guard.

Background

The federal government recognizes Indian tribes as distinct, independent political communities with inherent powers of self-government that include enacting substantive law over internal matters and enforcing that law in their own forums.[10] The United States has a trust responsibility to federally recognized Indian tribes and maintains a government-to-government relationship with those tribes.[11] The Bureau of Indian Affairs (BIA) within DOI provides law enforcement on Indian reservations unless tribes opt to assume responsibility for law enforcement or the state in which the reservation is located has criminal jurisdiction.[12] Federal crimes such as illegally crossing the border or drug smuggling across the border fall under the authority of federal law enforcement whether they occur on Indian reservations or not. However, tribal law enforcement generally has the authority to arrest offenders on Indian reservations and detain them until they can be turned over to the proper authorities, even if the tribe itself lacks criminal jurisdiction.[13] Further, tribal law enforcement officers

---

[10]See, e.g., *Santa Clara Pueblo v. Martinez*, 436 U.S. 49, 55-56 (1978); see also 25 U.S.C. § 1301(2) (defining an Indian tribe's power of self-government).

[11]The federal Indian trust responsibility is a legal obligation under which the United States "has charged itself with moral obligations of the highest responsibility and trust" toward Indian tribes. *Seminole Nation v. United States*, 316 U.S. 286, 297 (1942). The federal Indian trust responsibility is a legally enforceable fiduciary obligation on the part of the United States to protect tribal treaty rights, lands, assets, and resources, as well as a duty to carry out the mandates of federal law with respect to American Indian and Alaska Native tribes and villages.

[12]Under the Indian Self-Determination and Education Assistance Act of 1975, as amended, federally recognized Indian tribes can enter into self-determination contracts or self-governance compacts with the federal government to take over administration of certain federal programs for Indians previously administered by the federal government, including law enforcement. (Pub. L No. 93-638, codified as amended at 25 U.S.C. § 450 et seq.). In addition, Public Law 83-280, as amended, confers criminal jurisdiction over offenses committed by or against Indians in specific areas of Indian country on six states—Alaska, California, Minnesota, Nebraska, Oregon, and Wisconsin. See 18 U.S.C. § 1162(a). Tribes retain concurrent criminal jurisdiction over crimes committed by Indians against Indians.

[13]See *Strate v. A-1 Contractors*, 520 U.S. 438, 456 n.11 (1997) ("We do not here question the authority of tribal police to patrol roads within a reservation . . . and to detain and turn over to state officers nonmembers stopped on the highway for conduct violating state law."); *Duro v. Reina*, 495 U.S. 676, 697 (1990) ("Where jurisdiction to try and punish an offender rests outside the tribe, tribal officers may exercise their power to detain the offender and transport him to the proper authorities."); *U.S. v. Becerra-Garcia*, 397 F.3d 1167, 1175 (9th Cir. 2005) ("Intrinsic in tribal sovereignty is the power to exclude trespassers from the reservation, a power that necessarily entails investigating potential trespassers").

can be cross-deputized to enforce federal laws. For example, ICE designated a tribal law enforcement officer with customs authority and this officer provides intelligence to ICE and assists with ICE investigations.

DHS and its components have established a number of different offices to assist with facilitating tribal coordination on all homeland security issues, including border security. As shown in table 1, these components and offices have a variety of roles in supporting border security efforts on Indian reservations. Fusion centers, while not DHS components or offices, also support border security on Indian reservations by providing information to tribes.

Table 1: DHS Components and Offices That Support Border Security on Indian Reservations

DHS components and offices	Roles and responsibilities related to border security on Indian reservations
Office of Intergovernmental Affairs (IGA) Tribal Desk	IGA coordinates with state, local, tribal, and territorial governments regarding homeland security issues. IGA serves as the main point of contact between the Secretary of Homeland Security and tribal leaders across the country, and the Tribal Desk, as part of IGA, is DHS's designated lead for tribal relations and consultation.
DHS Office of Intelligence and Analysis (I&A)	DHS I&A works through fusion centers to provide tribal law enforcement agencies with strategic analysis of border security threats as well as facilitating coordination among tribes and ICE, CBP, and other federal agencies.
Federal Emergency Management Agency (FEMA) Grants Office	The FEMA Grants Office supports tribal border security efforts by coordinating with tribes to administer the Tribal Homeland Security Grant Program (THSGP), which provides grants for homeland security activities, including border security, and Operation Stonegarden, which provides funds intended to enhance cooperation and coordination among local, tribal, territorial, state, and federal law enforcement agencies in a joint mission to secure the United States land and maritime borders. There were no border security–related THSGP grants awarded to tribes for fiscal year 2012.
CBP Office of Field Operations (CBP-OFO)	CBP-OFO works with tribes to facilitate tribal members crossing the border at the POEs, none of which are located on Indian reservations.
Border Patrol tribal liaisons	According to a senior Border Patrol official, tribal liaisons are designated Border Patrol personnel at the sector or station level responsible for facilitating partnerships, improving relationships, and cultivating trust with tribal communities that have a nexus to the border.
United States Coast Guard (USCG)	USCG partners with the Border Patrol, among other DHS components, to coordinate with tribal, state, and local law enforcement to address maritime border security issues, such as conducting surveillance patrols of international maritime boundaries adjacent to Indian reservations.
ICE Homeland Security Investigations (HSI)	Besides working in other areas, HSI investigates immigration crime; human rights violations and human smuggling; and the smuggling of narcotics, weapons, and other types of contraband.
CBP Office of State, Local and Tribal Liaison	The CBP Office of State, Local and Tribal Liaison is responsible for establishing and nurturing relationships with state and local governments as well as tribal and territorial entities.

DHS components and offices	Roles and responsibilities related to border security on Indian reservations
ICE Office of State, Local and Tribal Coordination (OSLTC)	OSLTC is responsible for building and improving relationships and coordinating partnership activities for state, local, and tribal governments, as well as law enforcement agencies and groups.

Source: GAO analysis of DHS data.

DHS and its components also have strategies, as shown in table 2, that help facilitate coordination between DHS and tribes to address border security on Indian reservations.

Table 2: Summary of DHS Strategies Addressing Border Security on Indian Reservations

Strategy	Description of DHS strategy as it relates to border security on Indian reservations
DHS Northern Border Strategy, Issued by DHS in 2012	Emphasizes the importance of federal, state, local, territorial, tribal, and Canadian partnerships in achieving DHS's goals for the northern border. DHS's goals include collaborating to deter and prevent terrorism and transnational threats at the earliest opportunity, including before they reach U.S. borders; enabling the efficient flow of lawful trade and travel across U.S. borders; and the achievement of a border at which the nations' shared communities, critical infrastructure, and populations are prepared and protected through binational and bilateral security, resilience, and response protocols and activities.
	States that maintain partnerships with tribes across the United States and First Nations in Canada are critical in strengthening land and maritime domain border security.
2012-2016: Border Patrol Strategic Plan, Issued by CBP and the Border Patrol in 2012	Addresses coordination with the tribes on border security as part of its overall partnership with federal, state, local, tribal, and international partners in meeting its goal of working with all of its partners to secure the border using information, integration, and rapid response in a risk-based manner.
	Tribal coordination is also emphasized as part of the Border Patrol's international liaison efforts; disruption of transnational criminal organizations; and holistic, whole-of-government approach to securing the borders. Specifically, the Border Patrol is responsible for building coalitions with international, federal, state, local, and tribal law enforcement agencies; public service entities; and other identified stakeholders to develop a common operational strategy in the border environment.
U.S. Customs and Border Protection, Northern Border Strategy Issued by CBP in 2009	This strategy addresses tribal coordination as part of its overall partnership with federal, state, local, and tribal governments. As part of this broader partnership, this strategy calls for enhancing relationships with state, local, tribal, and foreign partners and leveraging intelligence and partnerships with tribal governments to address limitations in surveillance and response in some areas along the border.

Source: GAO analysis of DHS data.

Note: The Office of National Drug Control Policy (ONDCP) 2011 National Southwest Border Counternarcotics Strategy and 2012 National Northern Border Counternarcotics Strategy also address border security on Indian reservations by describing how federal agency coordination with tribes to address cross-border crime can be enhanced.

DHS Is Coordinating with Tribes on Border Security, but Could Strengthen Efforts by Establishing Agreements and Oversight

DHS and Tribes Use a Variety of Methods to Coordinate on Border Security and Report Positive Aspects of This Coordination

The Border Patrol is coordinating and sharing information with tribes in a number of ways to address border security issues. The Border Patrol and six tribes reported using one or more of the following coordination methods: Operation Stonegarden—a DHS grant program intended to enhance coordination among local, tribal, territorial, state, and federal law enforcement agencies in securing United States borders—task forces such as BESTs and IBETs, fusion centers, tribal and public land liaisons, and joint operations and shared facilities to coordinate on border security.[14] Border Patrol and tribal officials report that they share border security–related information through the BEST and IBET forums, and tribal officials reported receiving border security–related information from fusion centers. In addition, according to Border Patrol and tribal officials, the Border Patrol uses tribal or public lands liaisons to coordinate with tribes on border security. Another way Border Patrol and tribal officials said they coordinate on these issues is by tribal law enforcement using Operation Stonegarden funds to support daily coordination with the Border Patrol, including participating in joint patrols with the Border Patrol. In addition to these methods, the Border Patrol and tribes reported using joint operations, such as patrolling together in the same vehicles and

---

[14]Operation Stonegarden funds are intended to enhance cooperation and coordination among local, tribal, territorial, state, and federal law enforcement agencies in a joint mission to secure the U.S. borders along routes of ingress from international borders to include travel corridors in states bordering Mexico and Canada, as well as states and territories with international water borders. The Border Patrol's public lands liaison agents coordinate with public lands managers, including tribal officials, to foster better communication, increase interagency understanding of respective mission objectives and priorities, and serve as central points of contact within the Border Patrol to facilitate the successful resolution of environmental issues at a local level.

using shared facilities, to coordinate on border security. Table 3 contains more detailed information regarding these coordination methods.

Table 3: Summary of Coordination Methods Used by Selected Tribes and the Border Patrol to Address Border Security Issues

Tribal–Border Patrol coordination and information-sharing methods	Examples of coordination methods
Operation Stonegarden	• Officials from one of the tribes we interviewed stated that the tribe is a participant in Operation Stonegarden, which has been very effective from their perspective. Tr bal law enforcement officers and Border Patrol agents work together daily via Operation Stonegarden. Tr bal officials said that Operation Stonegarden is beneficial because it allows for regular coordination between tribal law enforcement and the Border Patrol, as well as additional officers to provide a proactive presence to deter illegal cross-border activity.
	• According to officials from another tribe we interviewed, all coordination with the Border Patrol occurs as a result of Operation Stonegarden. These officials stated that if this program were not in place, tribal––Border Patrol coordination would not occur.
	• Officials we interviewed from a Border Patrol sector with responsibility for border security on an Indian reservation in our review stated that conducting Operation Stonegarden with tribal law enforcement allows the Border Patrol to extend its patrols of the border.
Border Enforcement Security Task Forces (BEST) and Integrated Border Enforcement Teams (IBET)	• Border Patrol station officials respons ble for border security on one of the Indian reservations in our review stated that the station and BEST communicate with other federal agencies, in addition to providing information on seizures and apprehensions related to the reservation to BEST partners.
	• Officials from one of the tribes we interviewed reported that tribal law enforcement has received information from the IBET, as well as providing information to the IBET. For example, tribal law enforcement, via the IBET, was able to assist Canadian authorities with an issue involving tugboats crossing into Canadian waters.
Fusion centers	• Officials from one of the tribes we interviewed stated that the tribe shares information with the state fusion center and participates in daily briefings provided by the fusion center.
	• Tribal officials from another Indian reservation stated that they receive border security–related intelligence, such as daily intelligence reports, from DHS components via a fusion center. The tribe also receives reports from another federal interagency coordination center and provides information on border security–related arrests to the center.
Border Patrol tribal or public land liaisons	• According to officials from one of the tribes in our review, DHS and the Border Patrol have tribal liaisons and the tribe knows whom to contact regarding border security issues.
	• Officials we interviewed from a Border Patrol station responsible for border security on one of the Indian reservations in our review, reported that they use the public lands liaison program, which tribes participate in, to coordinate with the tribes.

Tribal–Border Patrol coordination and information-sharing methods	Examples of coordination methods
Joint operations and shared facilities	According to officials we interviewed from a Border Patrol station with border security responsibility that includes an Indian reservation in our review, joint patrols with tribal law enforcement are the most beneficial method the Border Patrol uses to coordinate with the tribe. These joint patrols assist the Border Patrol with developing plans and effectively utilizing limited resources to secure the border.
	Officials from one of the tribes in our review stated that tribal law enforcement conducts joint patrols with the Border Patrol, some of which involve Border Patrol agents riding in tribal law enforcement vehicles. This type of joint patrol is helpful because it allows tribal law enforcement and the Border Patrol to learn from each other.
	Officials from another tribe in our review reported that they use Law Enforcement Centers (LEC) to address border security threats.[a] The LECs, because of their proximity to the border, reduce the time it takes the Border Patrol to process apprehensions and seizures occurring on the reservation.

Source: GAO analysis of DHS and tribal information.

[a]Law Enforcement Centers are temporary, dual-use Border Patrol tribal facilities that are leased by the Border Patrol and used to respond to security threats close to the border.

In addition to these mechanisms, tribal and Border Patrol officials reported using other coordination methods, such as agent-to-tribal police officer interaction, meetings, and e-mails to coordinate on border security. For instance, although officials from two of the tribes in our review said their tribes do not use any of the coordination methods described in table 3, both tribes reported using meetings to coordinate as the need arises with the Border Patrol on border security issues. Officials from six of the eight tribes and 4 of the 10 Border Patrol stations we contacted reported that these methods of contact are the most beneficial for coordinating on border security. Officials from one tribe in our review reported that the timely sharing of information via e-mail is the tribe's most important coordination mechanism with federal agencies. Officials from another tribe explained that leadership from the responsible Border Patrol Sector regularly calls the tribal chairman to discuss border security issues, as well as holding frequent meetings. Officials from four of the eight tribes and 4 of the 10 stations we interviewed also reported that they communicate daily with each other.

Officials from some of the tribes and Border Patrol sectors and stations we contacted reported positive aspects of coordinating to address border security issues. Specifically, officials from five of the eight tribes we contacted reported having a good or effective relationship with the Border Patrol. In particular, officials from two of the tribes we reviewed, as well as the corresponding Border Patrol sectors and stations, reported that there are positive aspects of DHS's overall coordination with the tribes to address border security threats. For example, officials from one of the tribes explained that tribal law enforcement officers have a good working relationship with the Border Patrol and that the Border Patrol is the best federal agency they have worked with in terms of coordinating with the tribe. Tribal officials cautioned that while the tribe has a good relationship with the Border Patrol, the majority of tribal community members do not want any Border Patrol presence on the reservation and that the tribal community is very mistrusting of nontribal entities, including law enforcement agencies. Border Patrol sector officials—who staff the sector responsible for border security on one of the two reservations—stated that in addition to productive monthly Border Patrol–tribal leadership meetings and daily interaction between Border Patrol agents and tribal law enforcement, the Border Patrol was the first federal law enforcement agency invited to speak at tribal schools and community meetings.

Officials from one of the tribes in our review also reported that DHS and the Border Patrol at both the national and local levels are more sensitive to tribal concerns now than in the past and that the Border Patrol is willing to work with tribal law enforcement in sharing intelligence and keeping the lines of communication open. For instance, tribal officials explained that they have quarterly meetings with the Border Patrol sector during which the Border Patrol shares existing and future border security strategies with the tribe, including the decision of whether to deploy surveillance towers on the reservation. As a result of this interaction, the tribe, according to tribal officials, feels involved in the decision to potentially install towers on the reservation to help monitor and better secure the border. In the past, these types of decisions would have occurred without consulting the tribe, according to tribal officials. Border Patrol sector officials—who staff the sector responsible for border security on the Indian reservation—stated that the sector has never enjoyed a better level of communication or mutual understanding with the tribe and much of this can be attributed to the level of coordination with the tribe, particularly the regular meetings held between Border Patrol agents and tribal officials.

Government-to-Government Agreements Could Assist DHS and Tribes with Improving Their Border Security Partnerships

Although Border Patrol and tribal officials reported positive aspects of coordination, officials from seven of the eight tribes we contacted reported coordination challenges related to border security. According to tribal officials, the Border Patrol does not consistently communicate to the tribes information that would be useful in tribal law enforcement efforts to assist in securing the border. Specifically, officials from five of the eight tribes we reviewed reported coordination challenges related to not receiving notification and information from federal agencies, including the

Border Patrol, regarding federal law enforcement activity on their respective reservations. The following examples illustrate these coordination challenges.

- Officials from one of the tribes in our review reported that they are not given advance notification of Border Patrol law enforcement actions, such as independently patrolling the reservation or the deployment of undercover surveillance teams, occurring on their reservation. These officials reported that they would be in a better position to support federal agencies with border security efforts if they received information regarding planned federal law enforcement actions in a more timely manner. Border Patrol officials from the sector stated that the Border Patrol notifies tribal law enforcement of its own operations, as well as joint operations, which often involve tribal law enforcement, on the reservation. However, the Border Patrol does not provide detailed information on its patrol schedule and dates and times of operations, among other enforcement activities, to non-law-enforcement entities.

- A tribal official from another Indian reservation stated that there are numerous law enforcement agencies with different enforcement objectives working on the reservation and that there have been a few instances in which a tribal law enforcement unit and another federal agency were tracking the same suspects unaware of each other's presence. These situations, according to tribal officials, were problematic because the agencies were concerned that the overall operation would fail because of the lack of notification by each agency of its respective operations. Although a Border Patrol official with border security responsibilities on this Indian reservation was not aware of the Border Patrol being involved in such incidents, according to tribal officials, when tribal officials and the Border Patrol work together, they can complement each other and act as force multipliers by utilizing their respective resources. We have previously reported on the importance of deconfliction and coordinating to prevent law enforcement entities from unknowingly interrupting each other or duplicating each other's efforts.[15] Moreover, CBP reports that in some areas along the border, surveillance and response capabilities are limited, so the success of its border security initiatives depends on leveraging intelligence and partnerships with federal, state, local, and tribal governments.[16]

- Officials from a third tribe in our review reported that although the tribe provides information to federal agencies, these agencies do not consistently provide information, particularly information related to tribal members, to the tribe. For instance, in 2009, Border Patrol and a county sheriff's deputy responded to an incident involving two individuals who tried to illegally cross the border on tribal lands. Although the tribe was conducting operations in the area and could have responded to this incident, tribal officials stated that they did not receive information about the illegal crossing from the Border Patrol. Border Patrol officials from the sector with responsibility for this Indian reservation were not able to confirm Border Patrol involvement in this incident.

Further, according to Border Patrol officials, in some cases, coordination challenges with tribes have affected the Border Patrol's ability to patrol and monitor the border so as to prevent and detect illegal immigration and smuggling. Border Patrol officials from three of the seven Border Patrol sectors and 5 of the 10 stations we contacted reported coordination challenges related to understanding and collaborating with tribes within tribal government rules. Specifically, officials from two sectors that include Indian reservations and corresponding stations reported coordination challenges related to tribal government rules that hindered law enforcement in working together to secure the border.

---

[15]Deconfliction is the act of searching available data to determine if multiple law enforcement agencies are investigating the same target individual, organization, communications device, or other uniquely identifiable entity and, if so, of initiating coordination amongst the interested parties to prevent duplicative work or possible "blue on blue" situations (i.e., personnel from two or more law enforcement agencies unwittingly encountering each other during a law enforcement operation, such as an undercover situation). GAO, *Border Security: Enhanced DHS Oversight and Assessment of Interagency Coordination Is Needed for the Northern Border*, GAO-11-97 (Washington, D.C.: Dec. 17, 2010).

[16]Customs and Border Protection, *Northern Border Strategy* (Washington D.C.: August 2009).

- Border Patrol officials from one of the sectors with border security responsibilities on an Indian reservation in our review stated that the reservation faces border threats and is vulnerable, in part, because the Border Patrol cannot patrol as frequently as it would like to on the reservation. The Border Patrol is limited, because of tribal decisions, in the type of border security enforcement, particularly the implementation of visible countermeasures, such as mobile surveillance systems or integrated fixed towers, it can implement on the reservation, according to these Border Patrol officials. Further, these Border Patrol officials stated that some tribal members are opposed to the Border Patrol's presence on the reservation, which, because of the potential for volatile protests by these tribal members, impedes the Border Patrol's ability to patrol certain areas of the reservation, including a road in a major smuggling area. As a result of these issues, Border Patrol officials reported that the Border Patrol cannot apply all of its capabilities, particularly technology, to address border security threats and vulnerabilities on the reservation. Tribal officials from this Indian reservation stated that although the Border Patrol is not permitted to implement border security technologies on the reservation because of tribal community preferences, the Border Patrol is able to implement technologies and checkpoints just off of the reservation. Border Patrol headquarters officials stated that the implementation of these countermeasures off of instead of on the reservation adjacent to the border hampers the Border Patrol's ability to secure the border.
- Border Patrol officials from a sector with an Indian reservation reported that the tribe has negotiated with the Border Patrol via its tribal resolution process and other means to limit the tactical infrastructure the Border Patrol sector uses to support the border security mission on the reservation. For example, the Border Patrol is limited in the deployment of tactical checkpoints and must negotiate regarding the deployment location of vehicle-mounted radar systems.[17] According to the Border Patrol, in one case, a vehicle-mounted radar system had to be moved to a tactically less

---

[17]Tactical checkpoints may consist of a few Border Patrol vehicles, used by agents to drive to the location; orange cones to slow and direct traffic; a portable water supply; a cage for canines (if deployed at the checkpoint); warning signs, portable booths, and canopies; and portable lighting. Vehicle-mounted radar systems consist of camera and radar systems mounted on a truck, with images being transmitted to and monitored on a computer screen in the truck's passenger compartment.

advantageous position because of tribal concerns over its location on a sacred mountain.

According to the Border Patrol, the tribal resolution process for gaining approval from the tribe to implement border security countermeasures is difficult to navigate, which significantly affects the Border Patrol's ability to quickly respond to threats, and reduces the Border Patrol's presence on the border. The tribal resolution process, according to Border Patrol officials, includes several steps for soliciting feedback and approval for all proposed Border Patrol actions from all of the tribe's districts and communities. Border Patrol sector and station officials expressed concerns about individual community members, including those possibly involved in cross-border crime, being able to prevent passage of the resolution. These officials also stated that the tribe has changed the approval process without communicating these changes to the Border Patrol, which makes it difficult for the Border Patrol to adapt to the changes for both new projects and projects already under consideration by the tribe.

Tribal officials stated that the Border Patrol established temporary camps on its own initiative without gaining approval from the tribal real estate office, so the tribal officials had the Border Patrol remove the camps.[18] However, these officials acknowledged that the resolution process is lengthy and can be tedious for Border Patrol officials, particularly since the Border Patrol has deadlines it must meet to receive funding for projects. They also recognized that some of the tribal districts were not familiar with the steps required by the resolution process. As a result, tribal officials have established a tribal committee to ensure the districts and the Border Patrol better understand the approval process.

Given these coordination challenges, written agreements between the Border Patrol and tribes could provide a mechanism to help resolve coordination issues, such as the tribes' lack of notification and information from federal agencies regarding law enforcement activity on their

---

[18]Camps are temporary structures that include resources like tents and trailers to house Border Patrol agents responding to a surge of threat activity.

reservations, when they emerge.[19] We have previously reported on practices that can enhance and sustain effective collaboration, such as establishing common standards, policies, or procedures to use in collaborative efforts and the development of written agreements to document collaboration.[20] We reported that as agencies bring diverse cultures to the collaborative effort, it is important to address these differences to enable a cohesive working relationship and to create the mutual trust required to enhance and sustain the collaborative effort. Regarding the use of written agreements to document collaborative efforts, we have reported on the utility and benefits of written government-to-government agreements between U.S. government agencies and foreign governments or other sovereign entities to improve cooperation.[21] These agreements, in part, provide a legal framework for improving partnerships, facilitate information exchange, define tasks to be accomplished by each entity, and establish written assurances of each entity's commitments. A government-to-government agreement could help DHS and tribal governments to come together as partners to establish complementary goals and strategies for achieving shared results in securing the border on tribal lands.

Border Patrol headquarters officials reported that they have considered the potential utility and benefits of written government-to-government agreements with individual tribes to address border security challenges. In addition, DHS has entered into memorandums of agreements (MOA) with individual tribes on other security-related issues, which have benefited DHS and the tribes. For example, DHS entered into MOAs with

---

[19]A government-to-government agreement, such as a memorandum of agreement or bilateral agreement, is an agreement negotiated between two sovereign entities—in this case, U.S. and tribal governments—with the goal of achieving mutually beneficial outcomes.

[20]GAO-06-15 and GAO, *Managing for Results: Key Considerations for Implementing Interagency Collaborative Mechanisms,* GAO-12-1022 (Washington, D.C.: Sept. 27, 2012).

[21]GAO, *Nuclear Nonproliferation: U.S. Agencies Have Limited Ability to Account for, Monitor, and Evaluate the Security of U.S. Nuclear Material Overseas,* GAO-11-920 (Washington, D.C.: Sept. 8, 2011); *Afghanistan: Actions Needed to Improve Accountability of U.S. Assistance to Afghanistan Government,* GAO-11-710 (Washington, D.C.: July 20, 2011); *Money Laundering: A Framework for Understanding U.S. Efforts Overseas,* GAO/GGD-96-105 (Washington, D.C.: May 24, 1996); and *International Aviation: DOT Needs Better Data for Monitoring and Decisionmaking,* GAO/T-RCED-95-240 (Washington, D.C.: July 11, 1995).

individual tribes regarding the implementation of the Enhanced Tribal Card, which is a DHS program that allows all federally recognized tribes to work with CBP to produce a card denoting citizenship and identity that can be accepted for entry at the POEs. A DHS official from CBP's Land Border Integration Project Management Office responsible for negotiating these MOAs with the tribes reported that the MOAs were designed to protect tribal sovereignty, as well as describe the steps the tribes must take to produce a card. These MOAs, according to this official, are binding and protect both the tribes and CBP from expending resources on developing the card without assurances that the card will meet the requirements of the program.

Both Border Patrol and tribal officials reported that a written government-to-government agreement could benefit their border security coordination. Border Patrol sector officials responsible for border security on one of the reservations stated that the establishment of such an agreement explicitly describing the steps required to obtain approval for Border Patrol actions, including the tribe's resolution process and mechanisms for notifying the Border Patrol when changes are made to the process or approval requirements, could help resolve challenges for the Border Patrol in coordinating with the tribe. Tribal officials also reported that a government-to-government agreement could assist with resolving remaining coordination challenges by supporting overall coordination and ensuring that coordination processes are followed. Officials from another tribe in our review stated that they would also be receptive to an agreement that shows respect for the tribe and its practices, is developed with tribal participation, and involves senior DHS officials with negotiating capabilities. Border Patrol sector officials with responsibility for another of the reservations in our review stated that they considered pursuing an agreement with the tribe, but decided instead to actively engage tribal council officials, law enforcement officers, and community members in resolving issues, a course of action that has, according to Border Patrol officials, been effective in gaining the support of tribal leadership and law enforcement. The Border Patrol sector officials noted, though, that if agreements with tribal officials were pursued, senior DHS officials would need to be involved in the negotiation of any government-to-government agreements because tribal leadership officials do not view the Border Patrol, as a law enforcement agency, as the appropriate federal government representative for negotiating these types of agreements. Officials from both of these tribes emphasized the importance of tribal sovereignty and the need for the federal government to interact with tribes on a government-to-government basis. An assessment of the utility of written, government-to-government agreements between DHS and individual tribal governments to address and mitigate specific coordination challenges, particularly for tribes facing border security threats, could help DHS build on its tribal partnerships.[22] Further, agreements that are tailored to help resolve specific challenges, such as not receiving notification and information from federal agencies regarding federal law enforcement activity on the tribes' respective reservations could bring greater transparency to tribal government rules for the Border Patrol. Utilizing written agreements to help ensure the partners are working together to secure the borders could better position the Border Patrol and tribes to address their coordination challenges.

Establishment of an Oversight Mechanism Could Enhance DHS's Border Security Coordination with Tribes

DHS IGA and Tribal Desk officials reported that they have taken various actions to coordinate with tribes on a range of homeland security–related issues, including border security. For instance, DHS components, including the Border Patrol, have tribal liaisons who manage their components' tribal outreach efforts. The Tribal Desk, which is responsible for coordinating tribal consultation and outreach with the component liaisons, holds monthly teleconferences with these liaisons to discuss tribal issues and programs, according to IGA and Tribal Desk officials. DHS also has a Tribal Consultation Policy that outlines the guiding principles under which DHS engages with the tribal governments. DHS, according to DHS IGA and Tribal Desk officials, disseminated this policy to all federally recognized tribes and presented the policy at national tribal conferences. DHS's Tribal Desk, according to DHS IGA and Tribal Desk officials, is working with the tribes daily to address tribal issues and improve its tribal partnerships. However, DHS IGA and Tribal Desk officials reported that the Tribal Desk does not have oversight of the components' tribal outreach efforts, including border security coordination, because their role is one of a coordination mechanism. The Tribal Desk is aware of the components' outreach to the tribes, but it does not have the authority to track the effectiveness of such outreach to determine if the outreach is occurring and if any changes to outreach efforts are needed. According to DHS IGA and Tribal Desk officials, each component, including CBP, is responsible for conducting its own tribal outreach and is only required to report to the leadership of its respective components and is not required to report to the Tribal Desk on its

---

[22]Marijuana and cocaine smuggling, as well as criminals attempting to bring various contraband such as firearms and bulk currency across the northern and southwest borders are cross-border security threats that occur on Indian reservations.

coordination efforts. As a result, there is no department-wide oversight mechanism for ensuring the effectiveness of components' border security coordination with the tribes.

According to *Standards for Internal Control in the Federal Government*, controls should generally be designed to ensure that ongoing monitoring occurs in the course of normal operations and assesses the quality of performance over time.[23] Such monitoring should be performed continually; ingrained in the agency's operations; and clearly documented in directives, policies, or manuals to help ensure operations are carried out as intended. We have also previously reported that federal agencies can enhance and sustain collaborative efforts by, in part, developing oversight mechanisms—or mechanisms to monitor and evaluate their results—to identify areas for improvement.[24] Oversight mechanisms can assist with reinforcing agency accountability for its collaborative efforts.

DHS, in accordance with a 2009 Presidential Memorandum on tribal consultation, developed an Action Plan and corresponding Progress Report in 2010 that described various action items designed to establish regular and meaningful collaboration with tribal officials, and to monitor at the department level tribal partnerships to protect the safety and security of all people on tribal lands and throughout the nation. The 2009 memorandum requires all federal agencies to submit to OMB a detailed action plan of the steps the agency will take to ensure meaningful and timely input by tribal officials in the development of regulatory policies that have tribal implications. As DHS was formulating the Action Plan, tribes recommended, among other things, that DHS develop accountability and tracking mechanisms to ensure that the agency is responding to issues that are raised through tribal consultation. The Action Plan and its 2010 Progress Report call for the implementation of various action items designed to monitor and oversee DHS's tribal coordination efforts at the department level, including appointing a Senior Advisor for tribal affairs to provide policy advice and leadership on tribal issues and determining the feasibility and usefulness of establishing an internal leadership advisory council on tribal affairs. According to the Action Plan, this intra-agency council, staffed by DHS IGA and composed of officials from the department and components, would provide ongoing advice to the

[23]GAO/AIMD-00-21.3.1.

[24]GAO-06-15.

Secretary of Homeland Security on issues and policies that affect tribes, including border security, as well as bringing together DHS leadership from across the department's divisions and components to ensure consistency on policies affecting tribes. According to DHS officials, while DHS took steps to hire a Senior Advisor, the position was ultimately not sustainable because of staff turnover and a lack of funding for the position. DHS officials further noted that the position of Director of Tribal Affairs within the Intergovernmental Affairs office was established to help fulfill this role. Additionally, DHS officials reported that they did not establish an advisory council because of personnel limitations, among other issues. The implementation of such action items, or another oversight and monitoring mechanism, could better position DHS to assess the effectiveness of partnerships with tribes at the department level.

We have identified coordination challenges related to border security since the establishment of the Action Plan by DHS. For example, officials from seven of the eight tribes we contacted reported coordination challenges related to border security, such as the Border Patrol's lack of consistent communication of border security–related information with the tribes. As DHS was developing its Action Plan, it received feedback from tribes regarding the need to establish accountability and tracking mechanisms to ensure that DHS is responding to issues raised by tribes. For example, in summarizing feedback received from tribes, DHS noted in the Action Plan that tribal leaders expressed frustration regarding the expenditure of significant time and resources engaging with a federal agency only to see very little response or consideration of tribal recommendations. However, DHS does not have a mechanism to monitor and provide accountability for coordination efforts, as suggested by the tribes and the Action Plan, to position DHS to, for example, identify departmental and component coordination successes as well as areas needing improvement, including addressing coordination challenges that have remained since DHS obtained feedback from tribes in developing the plan. An oversight mechanism, such as one or more of those identified in DHS's Action Plan, could help identify and address these coordination challenges as well as determine which coordination efforts work well. Further, such a mechanism could help DHS enhance its awareness of and accountability for components' border security coordination efforts with the tribes and better look across the department to determine the progress being made and the improvements needed to more effectively coordinate border security with the tribes.

Conclusions

The nature and complexity of Indian reservations on or near the border, along with the vulnerabilities and threats they face, highlight the importance of DHS and tribes working together to enhance border security. The Border Patrol, in particular, is coordinating and sharing information with tribes in a variety of ways to address border security on Indian reservations. However, these coordination efforts could be strengthened. Government-to-government agreements with tribes to address specific challenges, such as federal agency notification to tribes of law enforcement actions occurring on the reservation, that have emerged between the Border Patrol and individual tribes could help better position the Border Patrol and the tribes to resolve their coordination challenges and better work together to secure the border. Further, DHS does not have a mechanism to monitor and provide oversight for its tribal coordination efforts—including border security—that would allow the agency to hold components accountable for effective coordination and, as a result, is not well positioned to identify areas of coordination needing improvement. We have reported on the importance of monitoring and oversight for sustaining and enhancing collaboration, and DHS's Action Plan contains action items designed, in part, to assist with its monitoring and oversight of its tribal partnerships. A monitoring and oversight mechanism could yield additional information and insights on the effectiveness of DHS's coordination with tribes, as well as help reinforce accountability when coordinating to address border security issues.

Recommendations for Executive Action

To enhance DHS-tribal coordination on border security on Indian reservations, including DHS's monitoring and oversight of these coordination efforts, we recommend that the Secretary of Homeland Security take the following two actions:

- examine, or direct CBP to examine, as appropriate, the potential benefits of government-to-government written agreements with tribes facing border security threats, and
- develop and implement a mechanism to monitor DHS's department-wide border security coordination efforts with tribes.

Agency Comments and Our Evaluation

We provided a draft of this report to DHS, DOJ and DOI for comment. We received written comments from DHS on the draft report, which are summarized below and reproduced in full in appendix I. DHS concurred with both recommendations. DOJ and DOI did not provide written comments to include in this report. DOJ provided technical comments via an e-mail received on December 7, 2012, which we incorporated as

GAO-13-352 Border Security on Indian Reservations

appropriate. DOI provided oral technical comments on December 7, 2012, which we incorporated as appropriate.

Regarding the first recommendation, that DHS examine or direct CBP to examine, as appropriate, the potential benefits of government-to-government written agreements with tribes facing border security threats, DHS concurred. DHS stated that more formalized government-to-government agreements between CBP and tribal nations should be developed for substantive issues. DHS further noted that written agreements, subject to legal review prior to signature, will memorialize both the issues and solutions. DHS stated that the DHS Intergovernmental Affairs office will work with CBP in the coming year to determine how the recommendation can be implemented. We will continue to monitor DHS's efforts.

Regarding the second recommendation, that DHS develop and implement a mechanism to monitor DHS's department-wide border security coordination with tribes, DHS concurred. DHS agreed that developing an agency-wide program could further enhance the interests of the tribes and the department for border security and many other programs. DHS stated that, in consultation with tribes, it will convene an internal group to discuss the feasibility of establishing a permanent program or an intra-agency oversight committee to address border security and other issues related to interaction and program delivery with tribes. This action, if implemented effectively, should address the intent of the recommendation.

If you or your staff have any questions about this report, please contact me at (202) 512-8777 or gamblerr@gao.gov. Contact points for our Offices of Congressional Relations and Public Affairs may be found on the last page of this report. Key contributors to this report are listed in appendix II.

Sincerely yours,

Rebecca Gambler

Rebecca Gambler, Director
Homeland Security and Justice Issues

Appendix I: Comments from the Department of Homeland Security

U.S. Department of Homeland Security
Washington, DC 20528

Homeland
Security

March 26, 2013

Rebecca Gambler
Director, Homeland Security and Justice Issues
U.S. Government Accountability Office
441 G Street, NW
Washington, DC 20548

Re: Draft Report GAO-13-352, "BORDER SECURITY: Partnership Agreements and Enhanced Oversight Could Strengthen Coordination of Efforts on Indian Reservations"

Dear Ms. Gambler:

Thank you for the opportunity to review and comment on this draft report. The U.S. Department of Homeland Security (DHS) appreciates the U.S. Government Accountability Office's (GAO's) work in planning and conducting its review and issuing this report.

DHS is pleased to note GAO's recognition of the Department's efforts to improve our government-to-government relations with tribal nations, including report references such as one from one of the tribes, "that the Border Patrol is the best federal agency they have worked with in terms of coordinating with the tribe." Tribes are an important partner in the Department's efforts to strengthen the homeland security enterprise, including securing and managing our borders.

DHS remains committed to tribal consultation and adhering to best practices in consultation, and is working to continually improve relations and interactions with tribal leaders. This commitment has included the creation of the position of Director of Tribal Affairs within the Office of Intergovernmental Affairs (DHS-IGA) and the formalization of the Department's first tribal consultation policy in 2010.

Additionally, DHS-IGA and the Tribal Desk coordinate monthly Component meetings and receive updates from Components on tribal activities, and work with Components to resolve issues and concerns brought to DHS by tribal leaders and others. While the Components retain responsibility for directing their own border security coordination programs, DHS-IGA and the Tribal Desk frequently offer recommendations, suggest solutions, and bring tribal concerns to Components' attention, as appropriate and warranted. DHS believes, as GAO indicates in its report that ongoing Departmental efforts have had a positive impact on tribal relations. DHS will continue to improve these relations wherever possible.

The draft report contained two recommendations with which the Department concurs. Specifically, GAO recommended that the Secretary of Homeland Security:

Recommendation 1: Examine, or direct CBP to examine, as appropriate, the potential benefits of government-to-government written agreements with tribes facing border security threats.

Response: Concur. DHS agrees that more formalized government-to-government agreements between U.S. Customs and Border Protection (CBP) and tribal nations should be developed for substantive issues. Written agreements, subject to legal review prior to signature, would help to memorialize the issues and solutions. DHS-IGA will work with CBP in the coming year to determine how this recommendation can be implemented. Estimated Completion Date (ECD): December 31, 2013

Recommendation 2: Develop and implement a mechanism to monitor DHS's department-wide border security coordination efforts with tribes.

Response: Concur. DHS has historically entered into negotiations, consultation, and outreach to tribal nations regarding border issues as well as other DHS-related policies and programs. Those negotiations have included tribal input on numerous occasions, field and headquarters consultation with tribal leadership, and continued work with tribes on a regular basis.

DHS agrees that developing an Agency-wide program could further enhance the interests of the tribes and the Department for border security and many other programs. DHS, in consultation with tribes, will convene an internal group to discuss the feasibility of establishing a permanent program or an intra-agency oversight committee to address border security and other issues related to interaction and program delivery with tribes. ECD: December 31, 2013

Again, thank you for the opportunity to review and comment on this draft report. Technical comments were previously provided under separate cover. Please feel free to contact me if you have any questions. We look forward to working with you in the future.

Sincerely,

Jim H. Crumpacker
Director
Departmental GAO-OIG Liaison Office

2

Appendix II: GAO Contact and Staff Acknowledgments

GAO Contact

Rebecca Gambler, (202) 512-8777 or gamblerr@gao.gov

In addition to the contact named above, Dawn Locke (Assistant Director), David Alexander, Frances Cook, Kevin Copping, Corey Guilmette, Eric Hauswirth, Linda Miller, John Mingus, Robin Nye, Jessica Orr, and Jerry Sandau made key contributions to this report.

GAO's Mission	The Government Accountability Office, the audit, evaluation, and investigative arm of Congress, exists to support Congress in meeting its constitutional responsibilities and to help improve the performance and accountability of the federal government for the American people. GAO examines the use of public funds; evaluates federal programs and policies; and provides analyses, recommendations, and other assistance to help Congress make informed oversight, policy, and funding decisions. GAO's commitment to good government is reflected in its core values of accountability, integrity, and reliability.
Obtaining Copies of GAO Reports and Testimony	The fastest and easiest way to obtain copies of GAO documents at no cost is through GAO's website (http://www.gao.gov). Each weekday afternoon, GAO posts on its website newly released reports, testimony, and correspondence. To have GAO e-mail you a list of newly posted products, go to http://www.gao.gov and select "E-mail Updates."
Order by Phone	The price of each GAO publication reflects GAO's actual cost of production and distribution and depends on the number of pages in the publication and whether the publication is printed in color or black and white. Pricing and ordering information is posted on GAO's website, http://www.gao.gov/ordering.htm. Place orders by calling (202) 512-6000, toll free (866) 801-7077, or TDD (202) 512-2537. Orders may be paid for using American Express, Discover Card, MasterCard, Visa, check, or money order. Call for additional information.
Connect with GAO	Connect with GAO on Facebook, Flickr, Twitter, and YouTube. Subscribe to our RSS Feeds or E-mail Updates. Listen to our Podcasts. Visit GAO on the web at www.gao.gov.
To Report Fraud, Waste, and Abuse in Federal Programs	Contact: Website: http://www.gao.gov/fraudnet/fraudnet.htm E-mail: fraudnet@gao.gov Automated answering system: (800) 424-5454 or (202) 512-7470
Congressional Relations	Katherine Siggerud, Managing Director, siggerudk@gao.gov, (202) 512-4400, U.S. Government Accountability Office, 441 G Street NW, Room 7125, Washington, DC 20548
Public Affairs	Chuck Young, Managing Director, youngc1@gao.gov, (202) 512-4800 U.S. Government Accountability Office, 441 G Street NW, Room 7149 Washington, DC 20548